SEW SIMPLE *embroidery*

Want the great look of high-fashion embroidered clothing and home accessories without the high price tag?

Well, grab your needle and floss and get going on one of our 17 designer originals. We've included all the tips, tricks, and techniques you need to customize almost anything. Even if you've never embroidered, your embellishments will turn the ordinary into extraordinary with lots of polish and pizzazz!

Everything you need to know begins on page 2.

Leisure Arts, Inc.
Maumelle, Arkansas

Each design has a Stitching Diagram, a Stitch Key, and a Pattern. Use the Pattern for transferring the design to your project. Use the Stitching Diagram and the Stitch Key to determine the type and color of floss, yarn, or perle cotton; number of floss strands; and type of embroidery stitch you'll need.

We used ten different embroidery stitches in our projects. Refer to the embroidery instructions on page 33 to complete each stitch. Also shown on pages 34-35 are examples of the stitches used in different combinations. Use these combinations for inspiration to embroider your own unique designs.

To change the size of a Pattern, divide desired height or width (whichever is largest) of pattern by the present height or width of pattern. Multiply the result by 100. Photocopy the pattern at this percentage. For example: You want your Pattern to be 8" high, but the Pattern on the page is 6" high. So, $8 \div 6 = 1.33 \times 100 = 133\%$. You would copy the Pattern at 133%.

Use one of the following methods to transfer the Pattern onto your project.

For patterns with accent stitches on top of satin stitching, transfer and embroider the satin stitch then refer to the Pattern for placement of the accent stitches.

Method #1:

Trace the Pattern onto tissue paper. Turn the paper over and use an iron-on transfer pen to trace over the Pattern on the back of the paper. Position the inked side of the paper on project. Iron image onto project; embroider.

Method #2:

Trace the Pattern onto tissue paper. Pin tissue paper onto project. Slide a sheet of wax-free dress-maker's tracing paper between paper and project with colored side toward project. Use a tracing wheel to transfer pattern onto project; embroider.

Method #3:

Trace the Pattern onto tissue paper. Pin tissue paper in place on project; embroider, stitching through tissue paper. Carefully tear away tissue paper when embroidery is complete.

Happy Stitching

Leaf Pillow

Stitch Key
use 1 strand of yarn

Stem Stitch

Fly Stitch

Running Stitch-
shown in photo

Red Heart®
TLC® Plush
Light Sage

Stitching Diagram
(Pattern on page 29)

Garnet Pillow

Stitch Key
use 3 strands of floss

- Lazy Daisy
- Long Stitch
- Stem Stitch
- Satin Stitch
- Running Stitch
- French Knot- wrap thread aound needle 2 times
- French Knot- wrap thread aound needle 4 times

DMC 309

DMC 961

DMC 3773

DMC 3011

DMC 3012

Stitching Diagram *(Pattern on page 25)*

Stitching Diagram (Pattern on page 26)

DMC 720

DMC 3777

DMC 3011

DMC 729

Stitch Key
use 3 strands of floss

- Stem Stitch
- Long Stitch
- Lazy Daisy
- French Knot

Floral Basket

Crimson Cloth

Stitch Key
use 3 strands of floss

Lazy Daisy

Herringbone Stitch

Stitching Diagram

(Pattern on page 30)

DMC 5284

Tropical Shade

Stitch Key
use 3 strands of floss and 1 strand of yarn

- *Feather Stitch*
- *Stem Stitch*
- *French Knot*
- *Satin Stitch*
- *Blanket Stitch- shown in photo*

Eyelash Yarn

DMC 469

DMC 433

DMC 838

DMC 780

Stitching Diagram

(Pattern on page 26)

DMC 309

DMC 961

DMC 3011

DMC 3012

DMC 3733

Stitch Key

use 3 strands of floss

- *Long Stitch*
- *Stem Stitch*
- *Lazy Daisy*
- *Running Stitch*
- *Satin Stitch*
- *French Knot- wrap thread aound needle 2 times*
- *French Knot- wrap thread aound needle 4 times*

Stitching Diagram
(Pattern on page 26)

Floral Shade

Gold Pillow

Stitch Key

use 3 strands of floss

- Long Stitch
- Stem Stitch
- Lazy Daisy
- Satin Stitch
- French Knot

DMC 729

DMC 3826

DMC 838

Stitching Diagram
(Pattern on page 27)

Floral Pillowcase

DMC 3012

DMC 304

DMC 3809

DMC 327

DMC 976

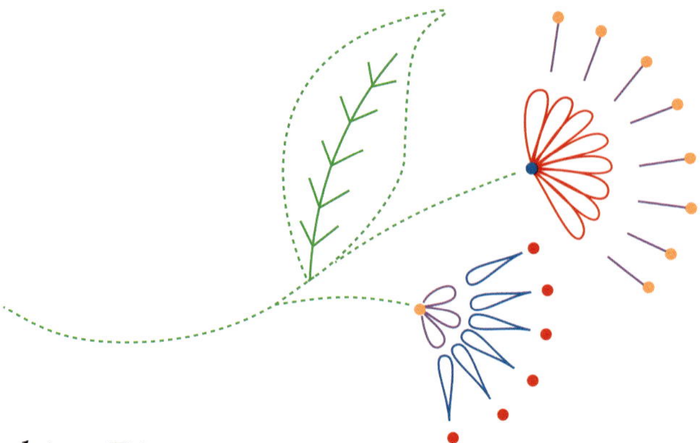

Stitching Diagram
(Pattern on page 28)

Stitch Key
use 3 strands of floss

- *Lazy Daisy*
- *Stem Stitch*
- *Fly Stitch*
- *Long Stitch*
- *French Knot*

Ecru Setting

Stitch Key
use 3 strands of floss

- Lazy Daisy
- Long Stitch
- Stem Stitch
- French Knot
- Satin Stitch

DMC 3836

DMC 3835

DMC 3012

DMC 3051

Stitching Diagram
(Pattern on page 28)

Blue Jeans

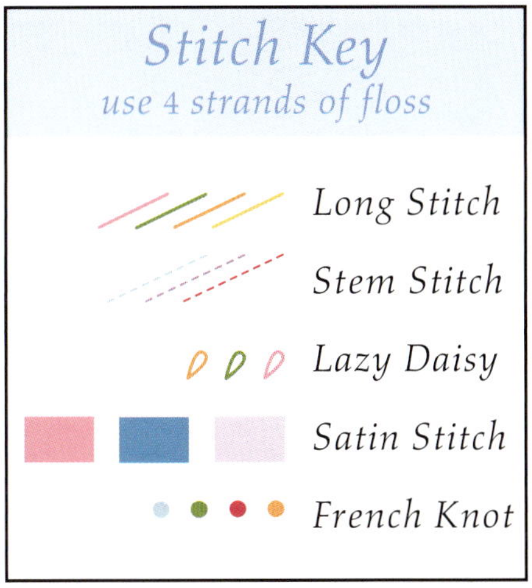

Stitching Diagram *(Pattern on page 27)*

Sailor Hat

DMC 553

DMC 971

DMC 602

DMC 3845

DMC 906

DMC 973

Stitching Diagram
(Pattern on page 29)

Stitch Key

use 3 strands of floss

- *Long Stitch*
- *Stem Stitch*
- *Lazy Daisy*
- *Satin Stitch*
- *Running Stitch*
- *Feather Stitch*
- *French Knot- wrap thread aound needle 3 times*

Denim Purse

Stitching Diagram
(Pattern on page 30)

Stitch Key
use 6 strands of 3753 and 3 strands of all others

- Long Stitch
- Stem Stitch
- Satin Stitch
- French Knot

DMC 312

DMC 3753

DMC 3011

DMC Ecru

DMC 433

Daisy Jacket

Stitch Key
use 4 strands of floss

- Long Stitch
- Stem Stitch
- Lazy Daisy
- Herringbone Stitch
- French Knot
- Fly Stitch
- Satin Stitch

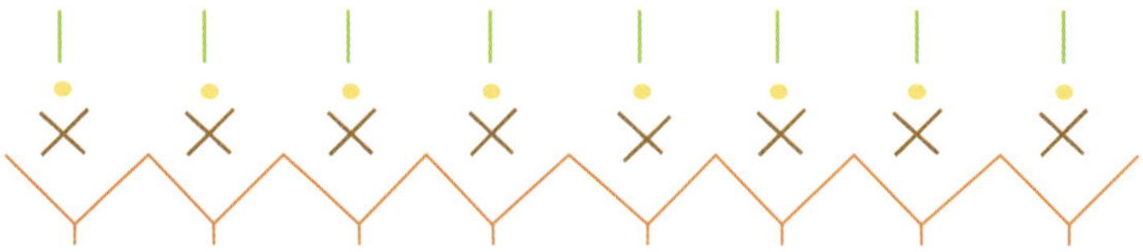

Stitching Diagrams
(Patterns on pages 30-31)

Straw Hat

Stitch Key
use 1 strand of perle cotton

- *Fly Stitch*
- *Stem Stitch*
- *Lazy Daisy*
- *French Knot*
- *Long Stitch*

DMC #5
Perle Cotton 971

DMC #5
Perle Cotton 703

DMC #5
Perle Cotton 726

DMC #5
Perle Cotton 988

DMC #5 Perle Cotton Variegated

Stitching Diagram *(Pattern on page 32)*

DMC Perle Cotton 971

DMC Perle Cotton 726

DMC Perle Cotton 703

Stitching Diagram
(Pattern on page 31)

Stitch Key
use 1 strand of perle cotton

- *Long Stitch*
- *Stem Stitch*
- *Feather Stitch*
- *French Knot*

Spring Sweater

Linen Shirt

Stitching Diagram *(Pattern on page 32)*

Stitch Key
use 3 strands of floss

- French Knot
- Lazy Daisy
- Feather Stitch
- Stem Stitch

Beige Purse

Bernat® Sox Hot Pink Yarn

Patons® Twister Fruit Loops Yarn

Garnet Pillow

Floral Basket

Tropical Shade

Floral Shade

Gold Pillow & Blue Jeans

Floral Pillowcase

Ecru Setting

Leaf Pillow

Sailor Hat

Denim Purse

Daisy Jacket & Crimson Cloth

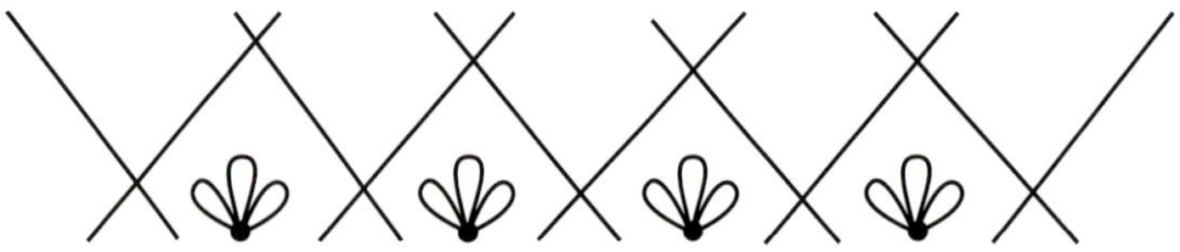

Daisy Jacket

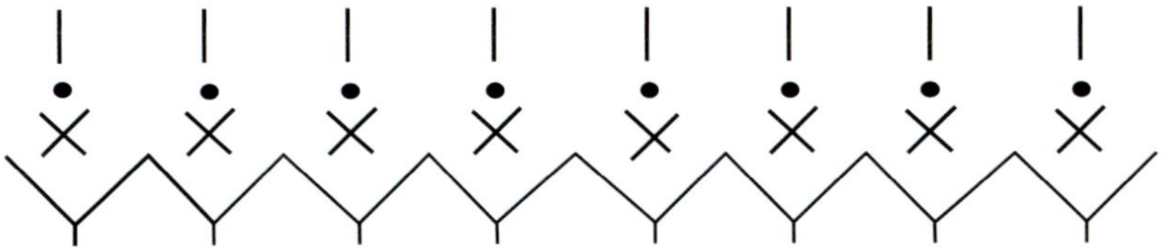

Spring Sweater

Straw Hat

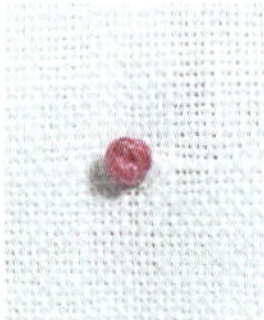

Linen Shirt

Follow the stitch diagrams to bring the needle up at odd numbers and down at even numbers.

Herringbone Stitch

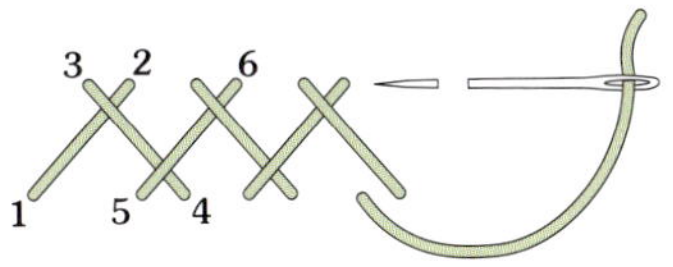

Bring needle up at 1; go down at 2. Bring up at 3 and pull through; go down at 4.

Feather Stitch

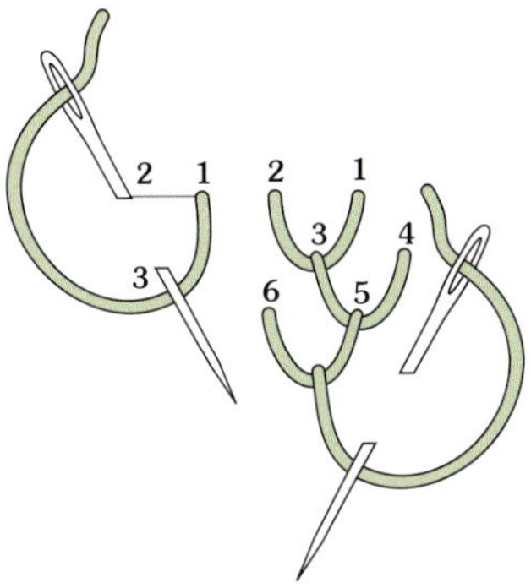

Bring needle up at 1 and down at 2, forming a "U" shape. Bring needle up at 3 inside stitch formed and then down forming another "U". End Feather Stitches by bringing needle up through last loop and straight down outside of loop.

Fly Stitch

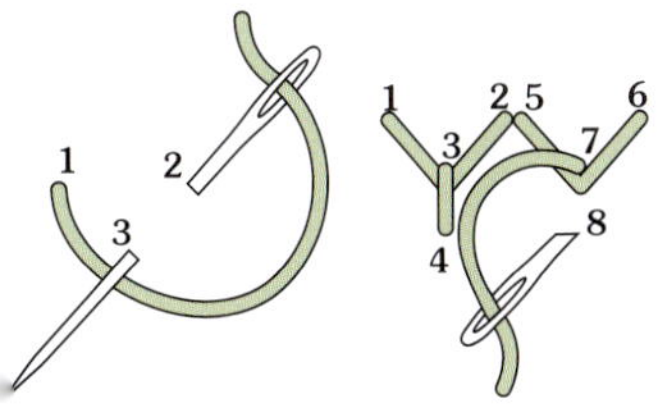

Bring needle up at 1 and down at 2, forming a "V" shape. Bring needle up at 3 inside stitch formed and then down on outside of stitch.

Stem Stitch

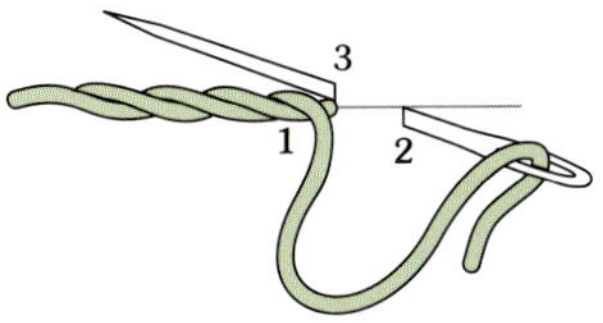

Bring needle up at 1; go down at 2. Bring up at 3 and pull through.

Lazy Daisy Stitch

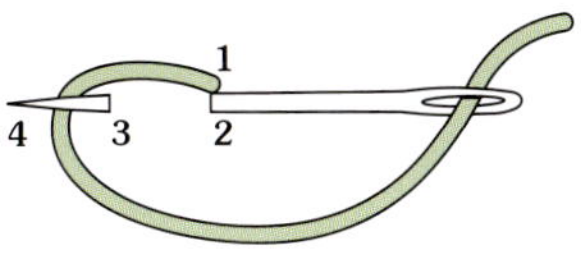

Bring needle up at 1; take needle down at 2 to form a loop and bring needle up at 3. Keeping loop below point of needle, take needle down at 4 to anchor loop.

French Knot

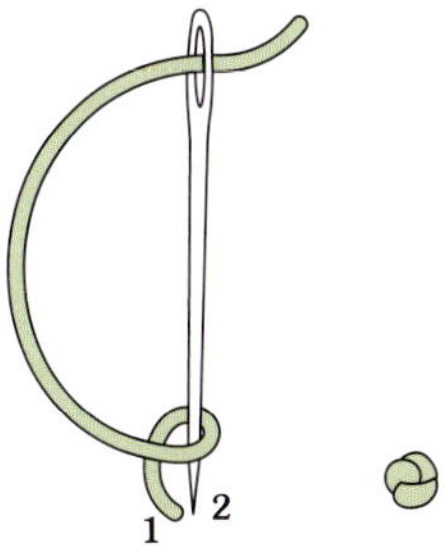

Bring needle up at 1. Wrap floss once around needle and insert needle at 2, holding end of floss with non-stitching fingers. Tighten knot, then pull needle through fabric, holding floss until it must be released. For a larger knot, wrap floss around needle more times.

Long Stitch

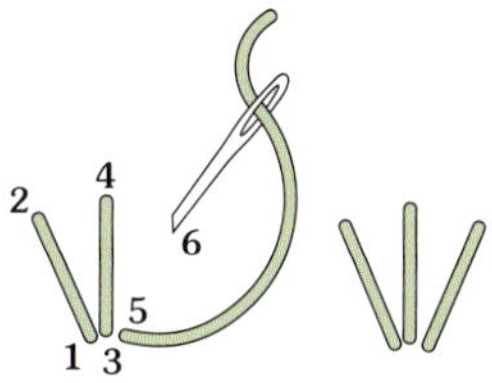

Bring needle up at 1 and down at 2. Length of stitches may be varied as desired.

Satin Stitch

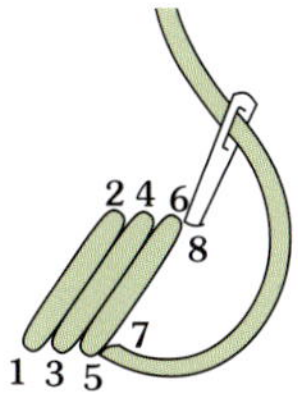

Bring needle up at odd numbers and go down at even numbers with stitches touching but not overlapping.

Blanket Stitch

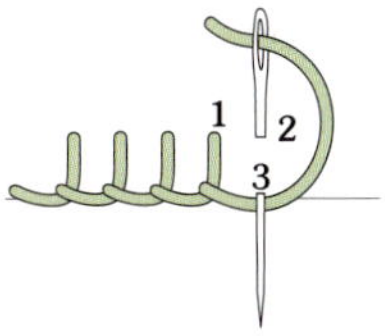

Bring needle up at 1. Keeping thread below point of needle, go down at 2 and up at 3 and pull through.

Running Stitch

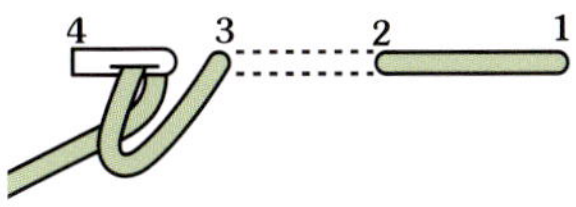

Make a series of straight stitches with a stitch length equal to the space between stitches.

Be Creative!

Combine various stitches to create your own unique look.

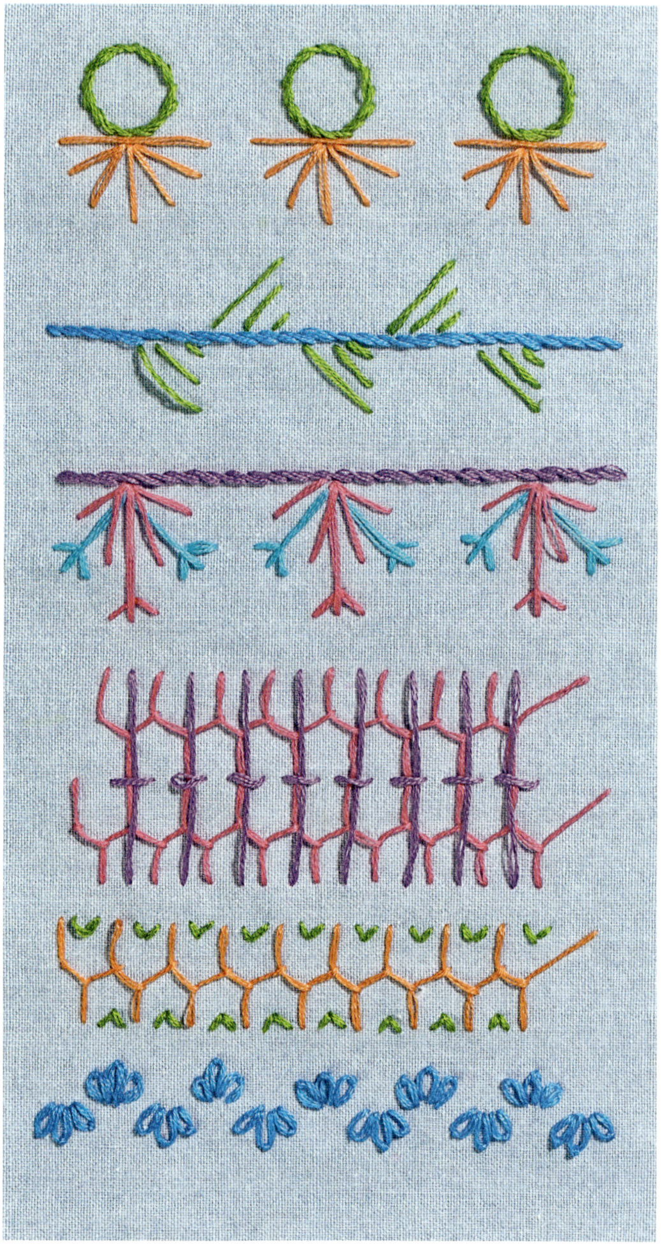

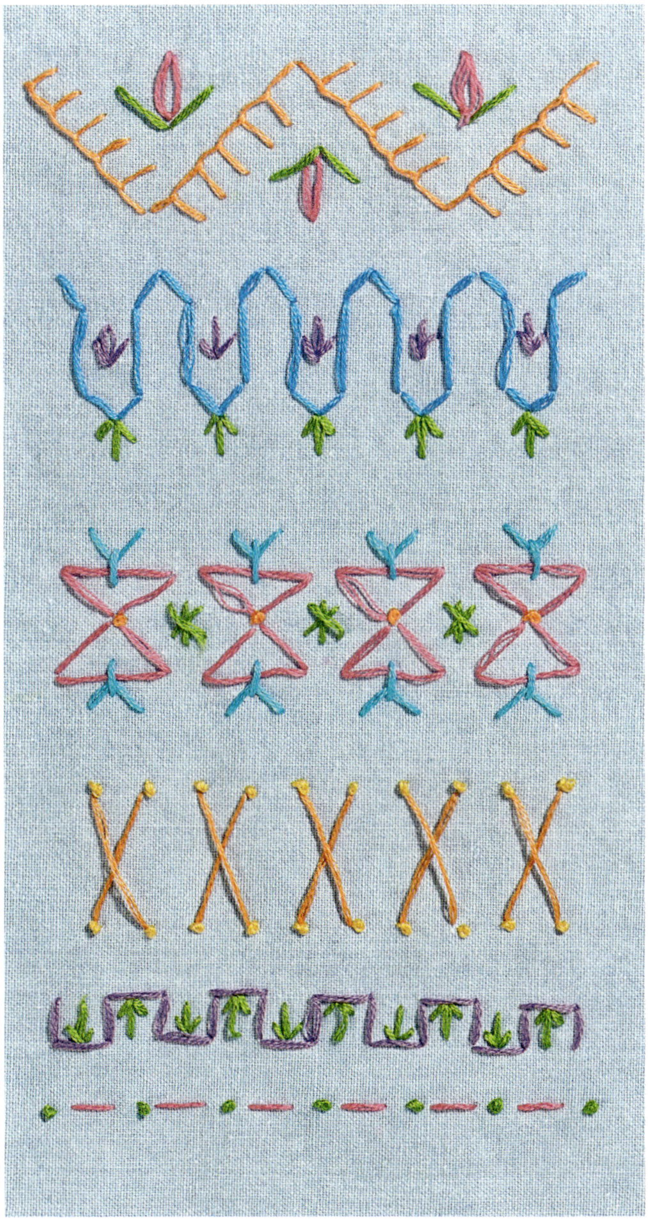

Credits

Production Team:

•Designer:
Patti Uhiren

•Technical Writer:
Joyce Scott Holland

•Graphic Artist:
Laura Adkins

•Photostylist:
Janna Laughlin

•Pattern Testers:
Nelwyn D. Gray and
Donna L. Overman

Embroidery floss provided courtesy of The DMC Corporation.